VERMONT DEPARTMENT OF LIBRARIES
NORTHEAST REGIONAL LIBRARY
23 TILTON ROAD
ST JOHNSBURY VT 05819

THE KILLER WHALE

BY LYNN M. STONE

EDITED BY
DR. HOWARD SCHROEDER
Professor in Reading and Language Arts
Dept. of Elementary Education
Mankato State University

PRODUCED AND DESIGNED BY
BAKER STREET PRODUCTIONS
Mankato, MN

CRESTWOOD HOUSE
Mankato, Minnesota

LIBRARY OF CONGRESS CATALOGING IN PUBLICATION DATA

Stone, Lynn M.
  The killer whale.

  (Wildlife, habits & habitat)
  Produced and designed by Baker Street Productions.
  SUMMARY: Describes the physical characteristics, habitats, and behavior of one of the few marine mammals that eats other warm-blooded animals.
  1. Killer whale--Juvenile literature. (1. Killer whale. 2. Whales.) I. Schroeder, Howard. II. Baker Street Productions. III. Title. IV. Series.
QL737.C432S76 1987   599.5'3   86-32884
ISBN 0-89686-323-9

International Standard Book Number:	Library of Congress Catalog Card Number:
Library Binding 0-89686-323-9	86-32884

ILLUSTRATION CREDITS:
Cover Photo: Jeff Foott/Tom Stack & Associates:
Tom Stack/Tom Stack & Associates: 4, 9, 18, 31, 35, 38
Flip Nicklin/Ocean Images, Inc.: 6
Rosemary Chastney/Ocean Images, Inc.: 10, 45
Alan D. Briere/Tom Stack & Associates: 12
Jeff Foott/Tom Stack & Associates: 13, 14, 24-25, 36
Al Giddings/Ocean Images, Inc.: 15
Bob Williams: 17, 22
Phil & Loretta Hermann: 20, 32, 41
Gary R. Zahm/DRK Photo: 27
Terry Thompson/Ocean Images, Inc.: 28

Copyright© 1987 by CRESTWOOD HOUSE, Inc. All rights reserved. No part of this book may be reproduced in any form without written permission from the publisher, except for brief passages included in a review. Printed in the United States of America.

Hwy. 66 South, Box 3427
Mankato, MN 56002-3427

TABLE OF CONTENTS

Introduction: 5
Chapter I: The killer whale's family 7
    Cetaceans: The whales
    Adapting to life at sea
    The family tree
    A killer whale's senses
    The largest delphinids
Chapter II: Killer whale behavior 21
    A seafood diet
    Life in a pod
    Raising killer whale calves
    Killer whale communication
    Smart animals?
    Are they man killers?
    Range of the killer whale
    Life at the top
Chapter III: Killer whales in captivity 39
    A sea of controversy
    Life in oceanariums
    A first for Sea World
    Whale Watching
Chapter IV: The outlook for next century 44
    Safety for killer whales: The MMPA
    The future of killer whales
Map 46
Index/Glossary 47

A killer whale sends water in all directions as it performs.

INTRODUCTION:

Chad and his two friends, Greg and Justin, squealed with delight. In the huge tank in front of them, a sleek, giant animal surged out of the water and into the air. A man in a tight rubber suit was riding the animal! The boys thought it was the biggest fish they had ever seen. It was also the first one they had seen with a man riding on it!

The animal's "flight" lasted just a moment. It ended with a great splash. Water showered the three boys and everyone else nearby. "Mom, mom!" Chad said, a bit short of breath. "Did you see that black and white fish?"

Chad's mom laughed, wiping the sudden shower from her eyes. "Yes," she said, "I saw it, but it wasn't a fish that you saw."

Chad's friend, Justin, wasn't so sure. "I saw its fins," he said.

"Yes, it had fins all right," Chad's mom said. "But what you saw was a killer whale."

Just then the whale leaped and splashed everyone again. The boys were drenched, but the water hadn't stopped their questions. "If whales aren't fish, how come they've got fins?" Greg asked.

"Well," Chad's mom explained, "fish aren't the only animals with fins. Whales have fins, too. The animal that you just saw—the one that just splashed us—is a mammal, just as your dog is a mammal. Whales, like your dog, breathe air. They can't just stay underwater like fish can. Whales are like people. When you go swimming, you're in the water, but you still come up to breathe air.''

All three boys thought about that for a moment. They agreed that when they swam they had to come up for air.

''That killer whale,'' Chad's mom continued, ''is really more like you than like a fish. When you swim your body temperature stays the same, just as the killer whale's does. That's because people, like killer whales are mammals. Mammals keep a steady body temperature. If we or that whale were fish, our body temperature would change with the water temperature. On cold days we'd be very cold and slow. On warm days we'd be warm and active. That whale is a lot like us for other reasons, too. But I think they can wait until we find some dry clothes!''

Killer whales, like people, are warm-blooded mammals.

CHAPTER ONE:

Chad and Greg and Justin had a close-up look at a killer whale. But that's not unusual now. Thousands of people see killer whales within splashing distance everyday in oceanariums.

People haven't always wanted to be near killer whales. For centuries, people believed that the killer whale should be killed or avoided. The general feeling was that the killer whale was bloodthirsty, and very dangerous. Fishermen shot them. Navy gunners sometimes used them for target practice. A U.S. Navy booklet warned readers that killer whales "will attack human beings at every opportunity." The killer whales became known as "sea wolves" in America, and as *Mordwal,* or "death whale," in Germany.

Until recent years, most things written about killer whales made them sound like monsters. Tales were also told of killer whales attacking boats and men. Even the Romans, hundreds of years ago, thought badly of killer whales.

Where killer whales weren't hated, they were often treated with great respect and some fear. The killer whale was one of the most common symbols taken by Indian tribes on the Pacific Coast of North America. Indian artists put killer whales on totem poles, hats, canoes, and dishes. The Indians believed that killer whales lived like humans in their own "villages" in the oceans. Some Indians thought that persons who drowned at sea became killer whales. Others believed that killer whales could leave the ocean and crawl onto shore, where they would become wolves. Above all, the Indians of the Pacific coast viewed the killer whale as the most powerful of their gods.

In the mid-1960's, a few killer whales were put on display in oceanariums. Suddenly the "bloodthirsty" killer whales did not seem so fierce. The captive killer whales were curious and playful. They liked being around people. Trainers jumped into their tanks and swam with them. They learned tricks and became the favorite sea animals of people who visited the oceanariums. Killer whales with names like Namu and Shamu became famous.

Cetaceans: the whales

Killer whales belong to a group of mammals called cetaceans, the Latin word for "whale." The warm-blooded animals we call whales, porpoises, and dolphins are all in the cetacean family. (There is also a fish called a dolphin.)

The cetaceans include two groups of mammals known as whale bone whales and toothed whales. The whale-

The teeth of a killer whale do look dangerous! A trainer feeds a killer whale at Marine World, California.

bone whales have no teeth. They grow to a very large size. They eat tiny plants and animals that they strain from sea water through "filters" called baleen, or whalebone. The largest animal in the world, the 300,000-pound (135,000-kg) blue whale, is in this group.

The killer whale, which scientists call *Orcinus orca,* is a toothed whale. Except for the sperm whale, the killer whale, or orca, is the largest of the toothed whales. Porpoises, dolphins, pilot whales, narwhals, and belugas are also toothed whales.

As mammals, all of the whales are air-breathing and warm-blooded. They mate, have young that grow inside

The killer whale has smooth skin that helps it move through the water.

the mother, and care for their babies after birth. Female whales produce milk for their young, just as land-bound mammals do. Unlike many mammals, though, whales are smoothed-skinned.

Most whales are very large. Even the smallest adult whales weigh eighty-five pounds (38 kg). Whales usually travel in groups. They bear their babies, called calves, one at a time. The babies learn to survive from the adults which care for them. They are streamlined and very fish-like in shape. Their faces, like masks, have fixed expressions. The whales have no way to show in their faces any feelings they might have. Instead of legs they have forward flippers and a flat, fin-like tail. They have large brains. But what really makes the whales stand out among the mammals of the earth is their choice of home: the sea.

Adapting to life at sea

Living their entire lives in the water creates some problems for whales. One problem is warmth. Normally, the killer whale and its family have an internal body temperature of ninety-nine degrees Fahrenheit (37 °C). They keep that temperature even in the Arctic and

Antarctic, where the water temperature may be a frigid twenty-eight degrees Fahrenheit ($-2\,°C$). Killer whales manage to stay warm because they have a thick jacket of blubber, or fat. Their heart and other important organs are buried deep inside the blubber. Like insulation on a house, the blubber keeps the outside cold away.

Killer whales have to be skillful swimmers, living as they do in a world of water. Their flippers, one on each side, control their direction in the water. Their swimming speed comes from the power in their tail, or caudal fin. The large fins on the tail are called flukes. A killer whale's tail works up and down. The tail muscle can drive the animal forward at great speeds. A fish uses its tail for the same purpose — forward motion. But a fish tail flips from side to side rather than up and down.

The huge fins on the tail of the killer whale are called flukes.

The large fin in the middle of a killer whale's back is called a dorsal fin.

The swimming speed of a killer whale, or any cetacean, is helped by its streamlined shape and smooth skin. If whales had hair, it would slow them down. Hair would upset their streamlined shape. With their rubber-smooth skins, whales can move through the water with barely a ripple.

Killer whales are able to go for a fairly long time without a breath of air. Like all whales, they have nostrils on top of their heads. The two nostrils in a killer whale connect to a single breathing outlet. That's the killer whale's blowhole. By having its "nose" topside,

A killer whale breathes through a "blowhole" on the top of its head.

a whale doesn't have to lift its head from the water to breathe. When the whale dives, the blowhole closes tightly. When the animal rises to the surface, it blows the warm, stale air from its lungs through the blowhole.

The moisture in the warm air forms water droplets when it strikes cold air on the surface. This puff of "fog" that rises from the whale is visible from long distances. Whales blowing out their stale breath have caused many alert sea captain to cry, "Thar she blows!"

Underwater, where they feed, mate, and retreat for safety, killer whales need to be able to hold their breath.

When the temperature is cold, the whale's warm breath forms "fog" when it meets the air.

15

Whales have large amounts of a chemical called myoglobin. Most whales have eight or nine times the amount of myoglobin that land animals do. Myoglobin carries oxygen, the gas which all mammals take from the air they breathe. Thanks to a large amount of blood and myoglobin, killer whales can hold more oxygen in their bodies than land animals.

The family tree

Just how, when, and why these animals of the sea developed is a mystery. Some scientists believe that whales were once animals of the land. Ancestors of whales, the scientists explain, had four legs like other mammals. They lost their hind legs thousands of years ago. Well, almost. Even today most whales have useless legs or lower body bones buried in their flesh. The flukes are not hind legs, but tail muscle. What were once front legs on a land mammal have become the flippers. If someone looked inside a killer whale's flipper, he would find the bones of an arm or foreleg. It has the same bone structure as a typical, four-legged mammal. It appears that some ancient ancestors of whales must have been able to live both on land and in the sea.

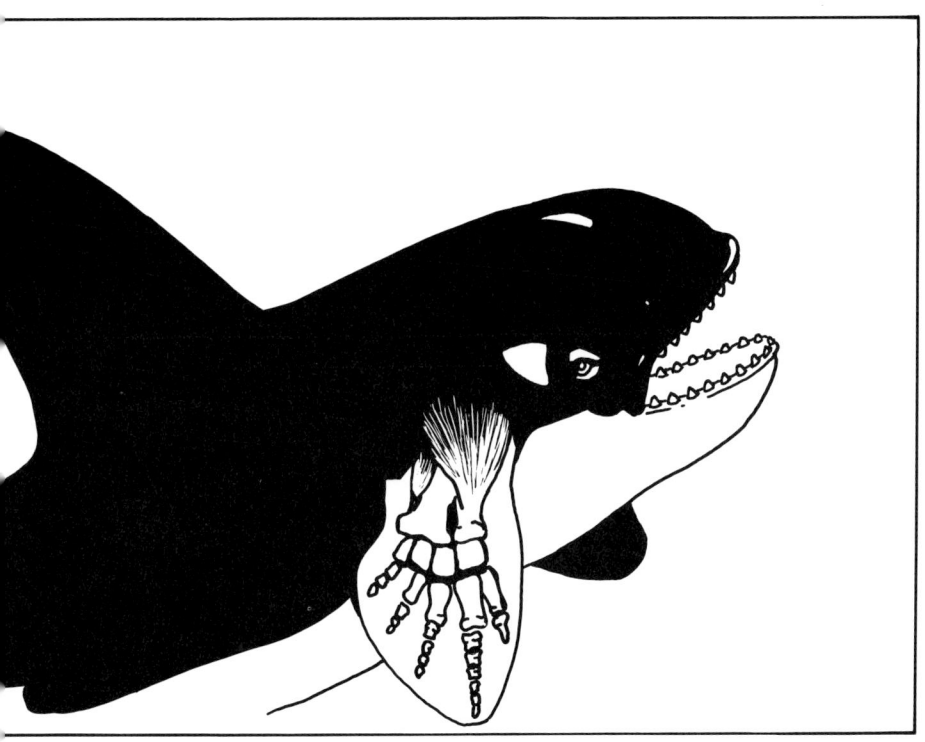

Killer whales have bone structures that are quite similar to other four-legged mammals.

Today, there are mammals that do live part of their lives on land and part in the water. These are the pinnipeds: seals, sea lions, and walruses. But these animals are much different from whales. The pinnipeds have body fur and four flippers. They come ashore to mate, have young, and rest.

A killer whale's senses

A killer whale will have no trouble seeing you if you swim with him. He'll see you well, too, if you stand on shore and he happens to raise his head from the water. All whales have good vision in and out of the sea. But in dark or cloudy water, even good vision is of little use. In deep water, where light does not reach, everything is dark. A killer whale's sense of smell is no help in deep water either. In fact, no whales seem to have a real sense of smell. They do have a fine sense of touch. The skin of a killer whale is sensitive, and the whales seem to enjoy contact with each other. Captive killer whales often find walls to rub against. Wild killer whales scratch on stones.

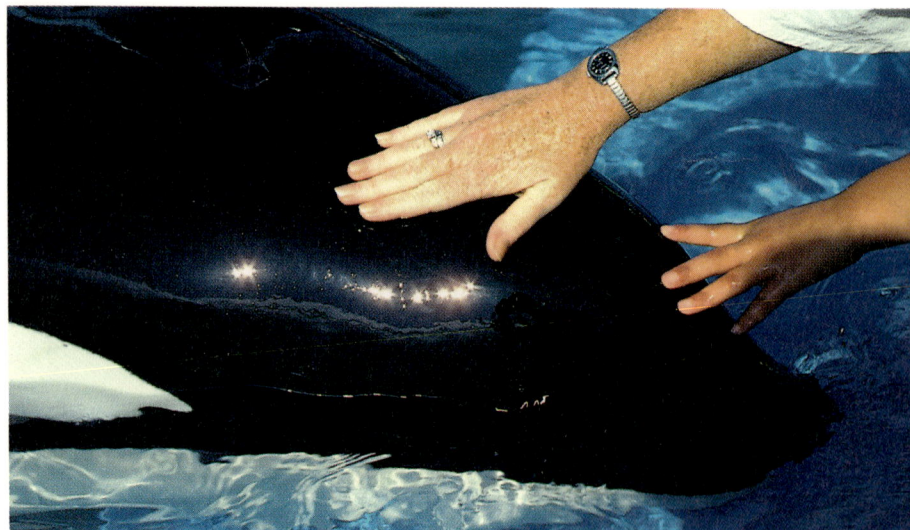

Killer whales seem to enjoy being touched, even by people.

The most important sense to the killer whale and its cousins, however, is hearing. The undersea world of whales is often dark and involves great distances. Killer whales locate food and each other by sound. The "ears" of whales show only as small holes on their heads. They are not big, but are extremely important.

The largest delphinids

Among the toothed whales is a group known as delphinids. The largest members in the group, like the killer whale, are known as whales. The smallest members are called porpoises.

The delphinids have many teeth in both their upper and lower jaws. In several species, including the killer whale, the teeth are cone shaped. They all have a notch in their tail flukes. Most, like the killer whale have a dorsal fin on their backs.

Killer whales are very beautiful animals. Their large size and beautiful color make them stand out from their cousins. Killer whales look like they were poured into tight, black rubber suits that are splashed and streaked with white.

Male orcas, called bulls, sometimes reach thirty feet (9 m) or more in length and can weigh up to eight tons (16,000 pounds; 7,200 kg). Females, called cows, may

Male killer whales can sometimes reach thirty feet (9 m) in length. Females, like this one, seldom are longer than twenty feet (6.5 m).

reach twenty-one feet (6.5 m) and perhaps five or six tons (10,000 - 12,000 pounds; 4,500 - 5,400 kg). Male killer whales have a tall, triangle-shaped dorsal fin. It can be six feet (1.8 m) tall! The female's dorsal fin is much smaller and sickle-shaped.

CHAPTER TWO:

Imagine being in the sea with a twelve thousand-pound (5,400-kg) black and white "bullet." It races toward you at thirty miles per hour (48 km per hour). That is the view of a killer whale that many marine animals in the ocean see only once—before they are eaten! A killer whale is faster than almost any animal in the sea. Its only speed rivals are the fin whale, sei whale, blue whale, and some small dolphins.

The killer whale comes armed with about forty teeth. Each of the teeth is pointed inward and measures about three inches (8 cm) in length. They are used to bite and tear flesh.

Killer whales travel in groups called pods. The members of a pod hunt together. Most often they catch fish. They sometimes hunt in a V-formation. At other times the pod spreads out. A scientist watched forty orcas hunt salmon off British Columbia, Canada. The pod slowly circled around hundreds of salmon. When the killer whales had forced the salmon into a fairly small area, they attacked.

Orcas have been reported to have knocked seals from little "islands" of ice. Killer whales are able to hit the ice very hard. A seal that has rolled from the ice into a pod of orcas has little chance to swim away.

A seafood diet

The killer whale's reputation as the "big, bad wolf" of the sea came from its eating habits. It is one of the few marine, or salt water, mammals that will eat other warm-blooded animals. Orcas sometimes eat sea birds, porpoises, seals, dolphins, sea lions, and penguins. But killer whales live mostly on fish.

The killer whale's diet differs from place to place. In some areas they eat squid along with their fish. Russian scientists watching killer whales in the Antarctic reported that orcas near shore ate seals. In the open

The killer whale got its reputation because it eats other warm-blooded animals.

ocean they ate minke whales and dolphins along with fish.

A pod of killer whales that lived all year in Puget Sound near Seattle, Washington, was never seen eating warm-blooded animals. But a pod that sometimes visited Puget Sound ate harbor porpoises. On the northeast side of Vancouver Island, British Columbia, killer whales swim with Dall's porpoises and minke whales. The porpoises and minkes show no fear of the orcas. Yet on the west side of Vancouver Island, orcas kill the same sea mammals.

Orcas have amazing appetites. A captive orca can eat 125 pounds (56 kg) of fish every day. Wild orcas are very good at filling their stomachs. One orca was reported to have the remains of twenty-seven porpoises and seals in its stomach! A man off the California coast saw a bull killer whale leap from the water with a full-grown sea lion in its jaws. That sea lion may have weighed six hundred pounds (270 kg).

Killer whales have been known to attack larger whales. But such attacks are rare. It appears that only whales that are old, sick, or pregnant are attacked. These large whales, such as the gray or blue whales, are huge. They may be two or three times bigger than an orca, but they do not have teeth to fight back. A pod of killer whales, attacking together, can cripple and kill any sea mammal.

Killer whales need fresh water. Their salty ocean home is no help. By eating flesh, the killer whale fills

A "pod" of killer whales swim near Vancouver Island, British Columbia, Canada.

its hunger and its thirst. Killer whales get water that is in the animals they eat.

Life in a pod

A killer whale spends much of its life in the company of other killer whales. The orcas hunt, rest, travel, and play together. They seem to help each other, too. Years ago a ferry boat near Vancouver Island struck a young killer whale. The captain of the boat said that the cow and bull "cradled the injured calf between them to prevent it from turning upside down." Fifteen days later it appears that the adults were still helping the calf. A woman had reported seeing two killer whales keeping a third one from turning over in the sea.

The size of a pod ranges from three to fifty whales. The average is probably ten to fifteen orcas. Marine scientists think a pod is made up of a family of related orcas. There are cows, bulls, and calves in a pod. Experts think that new pods begin when a cow and her calves of several years split off from a large pod. Scientists can keep track of pods, because each killer whale's dorsal fin has its own distinct markings.

Killer whales spend much of their time swimming near the surface of the sea. Sometimes one will jump completely out of the water. This leap is called

A killer whale "breaches," or leaps, completely out of the water during a show at Marine World in California.

"breaching." No one is sure why whales breach. The whale may be playing or simply testing its strength. It may be trying to communicate with other killer whales. The breach may also be for some purpose about which we know nothing.

Killer whales are almost always "on the go." But, sometimes they do stop and rest. They may rest for a few minutes or for a few hours. When resting, they stay in a tight group near the surface of the water.

When resting, killer whales will stay in a tight group.

Sometimes killer whale pods join together. This usually happens in the summer or fall. Scientists are not sure why these "super pods" form.

Raising killer whale calves

A newborn calf is eight feet (2.4 m) long and weighs about four hundred pounds (180 kg). It's a large animal at birth, but is quite helpless. The calf is born in water that is likely to be very cold. It must reach the surface right away for its first breath. Then, to nurse milk from its mother, it must hold its breath and go back under the water.

Killer whale milk is very rich. It is nearly half butterfat, and is very thick. Killer whales can not move their lips, so they cannot suck. The mother killer whale squirts her milk into the calf's mouth. The baby just has to hold on. The calf will drink its mother's milk for about a year. By then, it is twelve feet (3.7 m) long and ready for a diet of seafood.

Killer whales do not reproduce quickly. A female orca carries her baby for sixteen months. She may have a calf only once in ten years, although some have a calf every three years. With such low birth rates, killer whale pods grow slowly.

Killer whale communication

Pod members often need to "talk" to one another. Since being able to see one another—or anything else—is hard to do in the water, nature has found another way of helping them "see." This type of "seeing" is hearing! Killer whales communicate by making noises. Scientists think that all cetaceans may use sounds in a larger number of ways than any other animal. Sound travels quickly in water, and over long distances.

Killer whales also use sound to locate food and other objects in the water. They make high-pitched clicking sounds. The sound waves travel through the water. When they hit an object, the waves bounce off and return to the whale. The whale can tell the distance of the object by the time it takes for the sound to return. The whale can also tell the object's shape and size by how loud the sound is. This system of "seeing in the dark" is called echolocation. (Bats use a similar system on land.)

Scientists have recorded a killer whale's signals three miles (4.8 km) from the whale. They think whales may be able to hear each other at distances of up to five miles (8 km).

When the killer whale Namu was caught, he was put in a rope cage. The cage was slowly towed through the ocean to Seattle, Washington. During the towing, a pod

Killer whales "talk" to each other by making special sounds under the water.

of killer whales suddenly appeared. They charged the cage again and again, although they stopped short of contact. They had apparently answered signals for "help" from the captured whale.

Killer whales click, whistle, and "scream." Each pod has its own set of sounds. Some of the sounds are very different from those of other pods. Marine scientists have years of study left before they unlock the secrets of killer whale communication.

Smart animals?

Just as we don't fully understand killer whale communication, we don't really know how "smart"

Killer whales learn tricks rather quickly, and most experts think they are one of the smartest wild animals.

they are. They do have large brains, four times the size of humans'. They learn quickly, are curious, and seem to like to play.

Dale Rice, a whale expert, says, "There's little doubt that killer whales are intelligent—somewhere between a dog and a chimpanzee." But other experts say that killer whales aren't that smart. They feel that the view of killer whales as being very smart is in error. There is no proof, they say, that killer whales can reason, worry, or think things out like people can do. Still, their ability to learn, and their system of communication, places them among the smartest animals.

Are they man killers?

There is no question that killer whales are large enough to kill and eat humans. Killer whales are the largest eaters of red meat on earth. They are much bigger than great white sharks. They are eight times heavier than the largest flesh eater on land, the brown bear. Killer whales are twenty times heavier than the biggest tigers. But, are killer whales man-eaters? There are no proven cases of killer whales having eaten humans. There are, however, records of killer whales having attacked people. Such records are very rare. In the Antarctic, killer whales twice have swam up under ice on which men were standing. The whales seemed to be trying to roll the people into the water by smashing into the ice. Both of the men were able to safely leave the ice. The men may have been mistaken by the whales for penguins or seals.

A man in a black wet suit on a surfboard was bitten by a large sea animal in 1972. He later said the animal was a killer whale. The whale, however, did not continue its attack. This seems to be the first record of a killer whale attack on a human being in the water. But again, it's likely that the whale mistook the surfboard for a sea mammal.

Killer whales that have been shot or harpooned have attacked the boats that were after them. But no crewmen have been lost as far as is known.

In fact, wild killer whales seem gentle toward humans rather than fierce. Ted Griffin and his friends have captured many killer whales for oceanariums. When whales became caught in the capture nets, the men had to dive and cut the nets to free them. In their work, the men sometimes touched the trapped whales. They were never attacked. On many days, Mr. Griffin rowed a small boat among wild killer whales. The whales never attacked.

Marine biologists tell a similar story. The biologists, using small boats off southwestern Canada, studied pods of whales. The scientists could have been easily dumped into the sea by the frisky whales. ''The whales

Most killer whales are very gentle when around people.

did not disturb us in any way," one biologist said. "They merely seemed curious about our presence."

Range of the killer whales

Killer whales are found in every ocean. They seem to prefer the coldest oceans. In North America, they range in the Pacific Ocean off California to the Arctic Ocean and in the Atlantic Ocean off New Jersey north to the Arctic Ocean. North American orcas are most common off British Columbia and Alaska.

Just how much traveling killer whales do seems to depend on the pod. Some pods travel greater distances than others. Four pods of killer whales off British Columbia and Washington are always in the same area. Other pods seen in these Pacific waters come and go. How far they go when they leave the study area is unknown.

Many pods tend to travel toward the polar regions, either the north pole (Arctic) or south pole (Antarctic),

These killer whales stay near the coast of British Columbia throughout the year.

each summer. Some pods leave the icy polar regions in winter. Others live all year in the fingers of open water in Antarctica. Their rising blows of misty air can be seen throughout the year.

Life at the top

Wherever they swim, killer whales are the most feared ocean predators. Their role in the oceans is like the role of lions and tigers on land. Killer whales kill other animals in order to survive, as do the big cats. Unlike land predators, killer whales have a giant area in which to hunt. Often they live in coastal seas, near inlets and the mouths of rivers. The coastal waters are the home of seals, sea birds, and great schools of fish. Like all predators, killer whales must travel to where they can find food.

Killer whales are at the peak of ocean food chains. In this process, small creatures are eaten by larger creatures. It is called a "food chain" since one animal is linked to another. The Antarctic seas, for instance, are home for a small, shrimp-like animal called krill. The krill eats microscopic sea life. The krill become the main food for other animals, including certain fish. The fish that feed on krill are, in turn, eaten by seals. The fish and seals become food for an animal even higher on the food chain—the killer whale.

Killer whales have no natural enemies. They are at the top of the ocean food chain.

Being at the top has its benefits. The killer whale has no natural enemies in the sea. And, while no one knows for sure how long killer whales live, scientists agree that orcas lead long lives. Some scientists believe that killer whales live about thirty years. Others believe that the whales live to be one hundred years old!

CHAPTER THREE:

In 1949, the manager of the world's first oceanarium, Marineland in St. Augustine, Florida, had an idea. What if a porpoise could be trained to do tricks? He hired Adolf Frohn, a circus animal trainer, for the job. Within a few weeks, Mr. Frohn taught a two hundred-pound (90-kg) bottlenose porpoise named Flippy to leap into his arms. Marineland had its first star.

It was not until 1965, however, that killer whales were "put into the ring." And that happened more or less by chance. Two Canadian fishermen caught a killer whale in their net by accident. Ted Griffin, owner of the Seattle Aquarium, bought the whale, later named Namu, for $8,000. In Seattle, Namu was an instant hit. The whale attracted 120,000 visitors in its first two months. Meanwhile, the very fact that the Seattle Aquarium had kept Namu alive and healthy caught the attention of other people at oceanariums.

A sea of controversy

Since 1965, many oceanariums have put killer whales on display. But the idea of catching and keeping killer whales for public display is not popular with everyone.

Sometime after the capture of Namu, a group of killer whales died during a capture attempt. The public and news organizations were angry. Killer whales, once the terrors of the sea, had begun to enjoy a new reputation. The oceanariums had changed the killer whale's image. Now the oceanariums had their own image to worry about!

In 1976, a crew trapped a pod very close to the shores of Olympia, Washington. Many people were upset, and the state went to court. When the case was settled, strict limits were set for the future capture of killer whales.

Today, the capture of killer whales for aquariums or research is by permit only. Experts fear that capture of a whale may destroy the family ties of a pod. They also worry that the capture of some whales could drive others away from their favorite waters. So far, however, scientists don't really know what effects captures have on the pods.

Life in oceanariums

For a captured killer whale, life in a big tank has to be learned. Once the killer whale has begun eating well and seems relaxed, training can begin. First, the whale becomes used to the person who will be its first trainer. Then the trainer begins teaching simple tricks. Step by step the whale learns harder tricks. Killer whales seem to enjoy learning. Their reward may be food. More likely, their reward is doing something they like to do.

Killer whales seem to enjoy doing tricks.

41

The trainer may toss a new toy into the pool, or simply jump in with the orcas and play. Killer whales even enjoy being scratched by their trainers!

Training may be harder on trainers than on orcas. Sea World, for instance, keeps the water in the killer whale tank at fifty-four degrees Fahrenheit (12 °C). The water temperature is great for the cold-loving whales, but it's chilly for people. Worse, "You always smell like fish," a Sea World trainer said.

Training a killer whale is an ongoing job. The animals become bored easily, so the trainers have to keep them busy. But the results are amazing! The whales often carry their trainers like wet suited cowboys on bucking horses. The whale ride at Sea World takes a trainer from thirty-five feet (10.7 m) underwater to a midair leap.

Oceanariums like Sea World give their killer whales good care. Water is treated so it is as free of disease as possible. Vitamins and minerals are added to their food. The whales are watched closely, and have regular checkups from veterinarians.

No one is certain why killer whales become so tame. One answer may be a need for company, even human company. Wild killer whales are used to being with other whales in a pod.

A first for Sea World

On September 26, 1985, a baby killer whale was born in the 5,000,000-gallon (18,920,000-L) killer whale tank at Sea World in Orlando, Florida. It was the first healthy baby killer whale to be bred and born in captivity. In the future, perhaps all of the killer whales in oceanariums will have been born there. Then people won't have to worry about whether it's wise to capture wild killer whales.

Whale watching

Today, many boats can be seen among the whales in American waters. They are not there to harm the mammals. Watching whales of all kinds has become a popular thing to do. Trips to see wild killer whales are available in Washington, Alaska, and British Columbia. Some people even take tiny, one- and two-person kayaks to watch the pods of killer whales.

CHAPTER FOUR:

Safety for killer whales: The MMPA

In 1972, the United States government passed a law called the Federal Marine Mammal Protection Act (MMPA). It protected marine mammals, including killer whales, from being taken in U.S. seas. It also stopped importers from bringing marine mammals into the United States from other countries. The law does make exceptions. With special permits, a college or an oceanarium may capture a few marine mammals. The Eskimos of Alaska are not subject to the law, either. Eskimos are allowed to hunt marine mammals because it's part of their way of life.

The future of killer whales

The fat or blubber of whales contains a clear oil. The oil was once used both as a fuel and as grease. Soap, a type of butter, and cosmetics were also made from it.

Because killer whales are not nearly as large as other whales, they were rarely hunted. As the largest whales became rare, however, killer whales sometimes came under pressure. Not too many years ago a Russian whaling fleet killed 916 orcas in the Antarctic. Since then, the International Whaling Commission has made it unlawful to kill orcas anywhere. The demand for products made from whale oil is also not what it used to be. Populations of all types of whales seem to be increasing.

No one knows how many killer whales are in the seas. The National Marine Fisheries Service, the U.S. government organization that helps protect the whales, believes there are tens of thousands of orcas. They are in no danger of extinction. That's good news for both the killer whales and people!

Happily, orcas are not in danger of becoming extinct.

MAP:

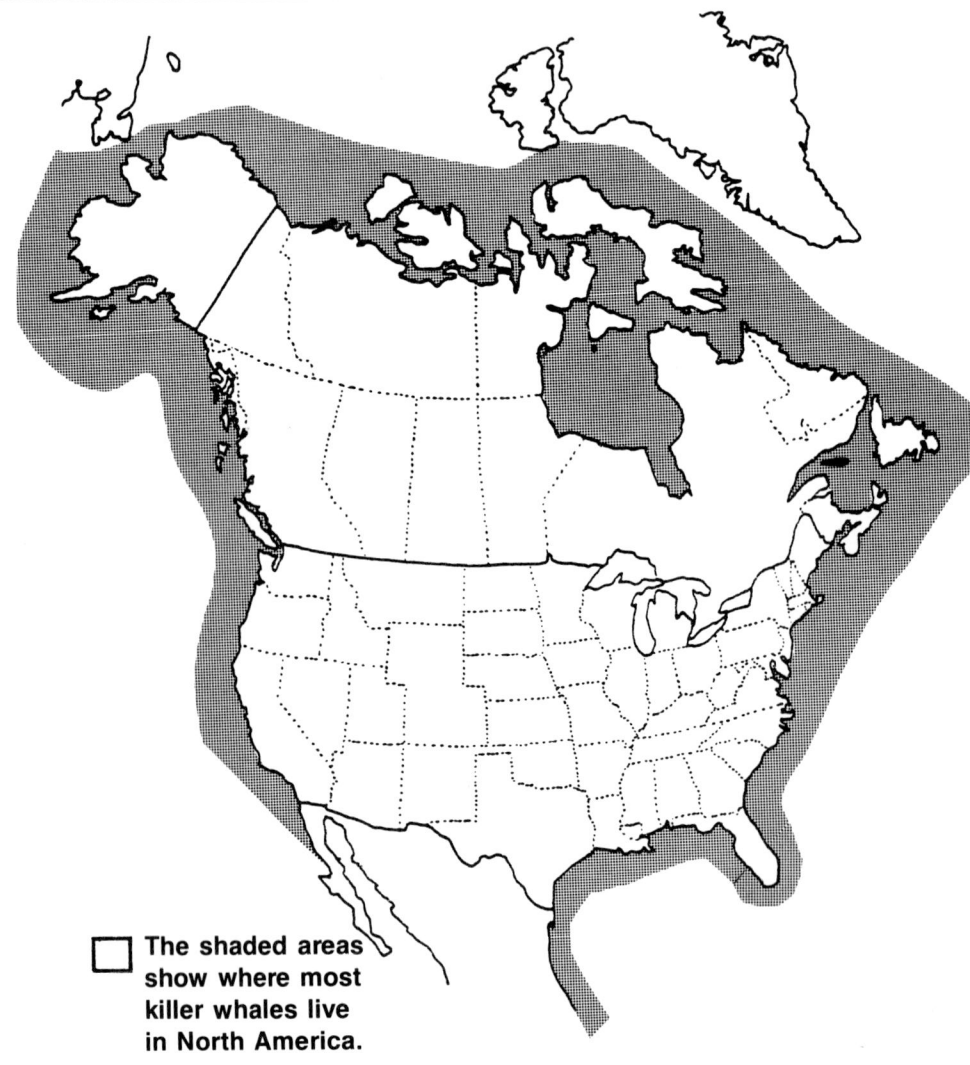

☐ The shaded areas show where most killer whales live in North America.

INDEX/GLOSSARY:

BLOWHOLE 14, 15 — *A whale's nostril, located on top of its head.*

BLUBBER 12 — *The heavy layer of fat in various sea mammals and birds.*

CAUDAL FIN 12 — *Tail fin, flukes.*

CETACEANS 8, 14, 30 — *Whales, porpoises, and dolphins.*

DELPHINID 19 — *Dolphins; a group among the toothed whales.*

DORSAL FIN 13, 19, 20, 26 — *The fin on the back of a fish or sea mammal.*

ECHOLOCATION 30 — *Process of locating objects by sending sound waves which echo back to the sender.*

FLIPPERS 11, 12, 16, 17 — *The fin-like limbs of sea mammals used to assist in swimming.*

FLUKES 12, 16, 19 — *A whale's tail.*

KRILL 37 — *Tiny, shelled shrimp-like sea animals; important food for whalebone whales and other sea creatures.*

MARINE 21, 22, 26, 32, 34, 44, 45 — *Related to the sea; the killer whale is a marine animal.*

MYOGLOBIN 16 — *A substance in muscles which works in the breathing process.*

NARWHAL (Narwhale) 10 — *An Arctic whale with a long, twisted, swordlike tusk.*

OCEANARIUM 7, 8, 34, 39, 40, 41, 42, 43, 44 — *A large aquarium for salt water plants and animals.*

PINNIPEDS 17 — *Seals, sea lions, walruses.*

POD 21, 23, 24, 26, 29, 30, 31, 34, 36, 37, 40, 42, 43 — *A group of animals of the same kind traveling or living together, especially whales.*

POLAR 36, 37 — *Related to the earth's poles, either north or south.*

PREDATOR 37 — *An animal which hunts and kills other animals (prey) for its food, such as a killer whale.*

WARM-BLOODED 6, 8, 10, 22, 23 — *Having warm blood, the temperature of which is controlled by the animal rather than by the environment; mammals are warm-blooded animals.*

READ AND ENJOY THE SERIES:

If you would like to know more about all kinds of wildlife, you should take a look at the other books in this series.

You'll find books on bald eagles and other birds. Books on alligators and other reptiles. There are books about deer and other big-game animals. And there are books about sharks and other creatures that live in the ocean.

In all of the books you will learn that life in the wild is not easy. But you will also learn what people can do to help wildlife survive. So read on!

j599.5
Stone, Lynn M.
The killer whale

DATE DUE		
N W r	MAR '80	
CC 4	JUN 86	
SEP 04 1998		
SEP 29 1998		

**VERMONT DEPARTMENT OF LIBRARIES
NORTHEAST REGIONAL LIBRARY
23 TILTON ROAD
ST JOHNSBURY VT 05819**

ABB-3871